Polish It & Publish It!

Henry Jordan

Published by Hank10 Publishing

Preface

So you have written a book, or maybe you have started a book but have a way to go to finish the complete book, and now you are pondering exactly how to finish it up and get it published.

You will find step-by-step instructions here -- including some tricks of the trade to help make your book not only professional, but unique.

Topics covered include:

- Do you need to get an agent?

- Must you do some or all of the work of formatting your book yourself for publication?

- Exactly what must you do to get it listed and sold by the major book sellers including Amazon, Barnes&Noble, etc.?

- What about E-books?

- Should you publish as a printed paperback, or as a printed hard-cover book, or as an E-book, or all of these?

- How do you get your book converted to be read on all the many types of E-book Readers now on the market?

- What are the differences between today's independent publishing and traditional publishing?

- Just what are your options in independent publishing?

- Which is right for you?

- What about digital publishing (Print-on-Demand) and E-books?

- How can you separate the truth vs. the shoddy advice from the hundreds of ads and claims you find on the Internet, all seeking your dollar but not necessarily accurate.

Read on!

Chapter 1

Then & Now

Publishing has changed dramatically. It used to be that a book author was considered to be "published" only if a large well-known publishing house in New York published the book. The publishers displayed their name prominently inside and on the cover of the book. Seeing the big publisher name gave the prospective reader confidence.

The Internet has changed the entire publishing industry. Today most people, with the exception of a few academics and literary snobs, don't really care who published it.

They just want to read a quality, interesting book.

An author can now become published without a literary agent, and without the big traditional publishing house, and feel proud of his/her book, if it is published as a printed book or an E-book, or both.

* * * *

For almost six hundred years, ever since Gutenberg's moveable type and the printing press emerged in 1440, printed books for sale to the public have been published and distributed mostly by a few large publishers. Mass marketing of printed books in the United States up to now has been dominated by a handful of publishers. As a rule, they have refused to read a new author's work for consideration unless it is presented to them by a favored literary agent.

Getting them to publish your book has involved correspondence, queries and exhausting efforts to find a willing agent, plus negotiations galore -- and a lot of just plain luck. Precious few authors make the cut.

Of those that do make the cut, many are astonished to discover that, once the Big Publisher has agreed to publish your book, you relinquish control. The big publishers take the copyright; then over the course of perhaps a tedious year or two of waiting, they edit the copy to suit themselves. They design the cover, they decide how, where, and how much, to promote the book, and they eventually print and distribute it.

If it doesn't sell right away, they simply discontinue the book, to the heartbreak of the author who poured months or maybe years, of body and soul into the creation of the wannabe masterpiece.

Authors take hope. Today a plethora of new-style independent publishing houses and self-publishing techniques are rapidly emerging, opening a whole new world for authors.

In the past *"self-published"* was thought of as *"vanity publishing"*, virtually a synonym for "No one would publish my book so I paid a company to publish it."

Today, self-publishing has become the choice of most new authors and many famous long-time, best selling authors. There is no longer any stigma associated with it.

Printed Books *vs.* E-books

Thanks to the Internet, E-books are proliferating wildly and giving printed books a real run for the money. Fresh talent is driving the industry.

It took automobiles forty years to replace the horse, and the CD took just fifteen years to replace the vinyl record, but it took only four years for Kindle E-books to overtake printed books at Amazon, the world's largest bookseller. E-books now outsell printed books at Amazon.

Printed books will continue to be the preference of many readers, but E-books are rapidly gaining acceptance and admiration.

There will be a market for both conventional printed books and E-books as time goes by. The eventual ratio of the two is yet to be determined, but the E-books have already captured an astonishing percentage of total readership, and that percentage is increasing exponentially every day.

Authors who choose to take advantage of the new technology, and personally supervise the publication of their printed book and/or E-book, can now follow the shifting winds of the marketplace and decide to produce books to reach one or both of the two markets.

Dozens of brands of hand-held E-book readers are on the market already, and more surface monthly. Amazon's Kindle triggered the rush. The Barnes & Noble Nook quickly became the number two horse in the race. Sony, Apple, Kobo, Diesel and others are striving to become the leader, or at least be a significant part of the crowd. Discount chain stores are seriously considering marketing their own in-house brands.

It is important to note that a large percentage of the population already own and use a device that can read E-books. Desktop, laptop, and tablet computers can read E-books. Many people are unaware of this since most of the publicity has dwelled upon the portable hand-held E-book readers.

Whether it be a laptop, desktop, notebook, PC, Mac, a tablet (such as the Apple iPad *etc.*), existing computers can be used to read E-books.

Smart cell phones can read E-books, although it is doubtful that many people will use them as such because the display screen is small and the text is tiny.

The trend clearly indicates that as time goes by, more and more of the general population will become E-book devotees.

Even the youngsters who have shunned printed books up until now are beginning to read more. Schools are beginning to endorse E-books. Libraries are gradually offering E-books for free or rental borrowing.

New Affordable, Rapid Publishing

Publishing is no longer a tedious time-consuming process. Independent publishing companies are making it painless and affordable for authors to get their printed books and/or E-books produced and distributed. Once you have finished writing, and formatted your manuscript file, you can get it published in a day or so as an E-book, and in only a week or so as a printed book. Expert professionals are available to help bring the book to market. Goodbye giant, cumbersome Big Publishers. Hello new, fun ways to get your book published.

Writers who found it difficult or impossible to get published by the big boys now find that they can publish almost instantaneously by utilizing E-book technology. For printed books they can utilize computerized print-on-demand services. This means they don't have to buy an inventory of books, hoping they will sell.

Getting your books sold, however, is a horse of a different color. It takes time, and it is not easy.

The independent publishers will provide "distribution" for your book by the large well-known distributors. That means your book is available from various sources. It does not mean it will be bought!

Making the reading public aware of your book has been the key reason the big publishers have succeeded. They print thousands of books at a time, publicize and promote them, and lean on the book stores to order them, stock them, and sell them according to the publishers' terms. The big publishing companies invest heavily in producing the printed books and making sure they are sold. Oh yes, by the way they remit meager royalties to the writer, many months after each sale is made.

Only a few authors hit the big time and make the big money. Their income is large because, although the royalty on each book sold is small, that royalty is multiplied by millions of sales. Most authors do not achieve such success. They must bask in the satisfaction of knowing and proclaiming that they are a published author.

To take the place of the big publishers' efforts to promote your printed book and get it into the hands of customers, today's author can get the book listed in the universal lists of books published, which all book sellers and libraries use. The author can also find the way to place his/her E-book with the E-book sellers, and put in place a system to fulfill orders from the book sellers. This system includes a procedure to process payments from individuals, book sellers, and libraries.

Fortunately all of this turns out to be straightforward. Getting the book listed and setting up a distribution system is the easy part. Convincing people to buy it is the hard part.

Most authors like to believe that once their book is published the world will beat a path to their doorway to get it and read it. Sorry! The public must be informed about the existence of the book, and motivated to read and buy it.

The librarians must be motivated to buy the book and promote it.

If the reader buys the book, he/she must be able to easily find it and purchase it. Book distributors and retail sellers for both printed books and E-books must be motivated to promote the book to their customers.

Your Book Must Be Good

It is vital to remember that, regardless of how your book is published, whether it is a conventional printed book or an E-book, your book must be good. It must be interesting, easy to read. It must be enjoyable and/or informative. The slickest sales promotion in the world cannot cause a poorly written book to gain acceptance and sustain popularity.

Word of mouth is what sells books. If people don't like your book, they will tell others. If they do like it, and post a review, other people will take notice and borrow or buy the book.

This book will guide you through the process of polishing your manuscript into a viable, attractive book ready to publish, and it will explain in detail the do's, don'ts and why's of putting that final polish on your book and how to actually publish it.

Chapter 2

Polishing It

You are proud of your work, and you believe it should be published for the world to enjoy. That is admirable, but have you stepped back and taken a truly objective look at what you have written? Is it ready? Is it professionally acceptable? Have you taken the two final steps to really get it ready for publication?

The first step is to go back over your entire book, with a fresh mind, as though you are reading it for the first time, and ask yourself three questions after reading each single paragraph:

Q1 - Did that paragraph make the story progress (*i.e.* did it flow)?

Q2 - Was it really necessary, or is it just a wee bit of showing how cleverly you manipulate words, in order to satisfy your own ego?

Q3 - Was it easy to understand, does it make sense, and was it devoid of big words that your typical reader might not know?

If you examine the best sellers and the classics, you will see that they follow these rules.

Esoteric Facts, Quirks etc.???

Many authors tend to get carried away with their stored knowledge of esoteric facts, quirks, and seldom-used words. They write for themselves, not for other readers.

Too often they write to impress other authors and a few literary aficionados. You might want to think about this as you go back over your manuscript with an objective frame of mind. You may want to simplify your copy by exchanging common words and phrases for esoteric words. You may find that eliminating one or more paragraphs in your book will actually improve it.

Make It Easy On The Reader

On the other hand, you may realize that adding a paragraph here and there, with more information that will help the reader understand what is on your mind, could improve the book. We all get carried away with our writing and sometimes forget that the reader does not know exactly what you are trying to get across unless you specifically write down the words that explain your thoughts. You have the whole book in your mind. Your reader doesn't. He/she reads one word, one line, and one paragraph at a time.

Each paragraph in your book must stand on its own, and it should not contain more than one chain of thought. Imposing a second subject into a paragraph is one of the quickest ways to confuse and irritate a reader, and to brand your book as amateur.

Ironically, it often makes sense to break one chain of thought into several paragraphs. Humans tend to get tired of reading long paragraphs. They like to think they can pause ever so briefly and take a mental breath when a paragraph ends, even though they may need the following paragraph to complete the message you are trying to convey.

Follow The Rules

Adherence to the rules of grammar, punctuation, and spelling are mandatory. Cutesy writing that violates these principles does not appeal to most people. Book sales are meager if the book tries to be cute instead of interesting and entertaining. The content should carry itself without the aid of phony tricks of grammar and spelling.

Vary The Pace

Don't forget to vary the pace throughout your book. Make it flow peacefully like a deep river at times, like a swift stream at other times, and like water rushing over rocks in rapids from time to time.

The reader can get bored by sameness. Surprise him/her every once in awhile by pacing your story with variations in how much and what type of information you present at a time.

As you go through your manuscript, by all means retain your creativity. Be yourself. Don't try to copycat Twain, Michener, King, Steele, Rowling *etc*.

Step Two is simple: Let a professional proof-read it.

You may pride yourself at being a meticulous reader, and you may have gone through your book many times to bring it to where it is now, but it is imperative that someone else carefully proof-read the book before you publish it. Preferably a professional.

If you have something that pleases or satisfies your reader, your book will be successful, whether it makes money for you or not. Your goal is to make it the best possible without beating it to death by putting off publishing forever in the hopes of making it even better. You can always write another book if you have more to say.

Follow the suggestions here. Then go ahead and publish it.

Chapter 3

Some Fundamentals of Good Creative Writing

All of us learned to read and write in school, where conventional strict rules and procedures were drilled into us by devoted teachers. Unfortunately, most courses in English grammar and literature did not focus on teaching creative writing. They simply gave us the rules and let us peek at what others have written.

In creative writing, you must follow two of the fundamental techniques of the three R's of course (Reading and wRiting -- you don't need much aRithmetic, the computer will count your words for you), but in order to be a true creative author, you must exercise your own unique creativity. It's as simple as that!

It is difficult to teach creativity. You must have it as intuition. However, there are some fundamental rules of the road in creative writing that can warn you of bumps ahead. There are some danger signs that you can learn to recognize. Here are some don'ts that will help you evaluate your work and guide your future writing.

Guard against long sentences in general. Many best selling authors advise us to use mostly verbs and nouns. They caution us to use adjectives and adverbs sparingly. Also, they advise active transitive sentence structure instead of passive description wherever possible. As a general rule, each sentence should be as brief as possible to get the point across. Often two or more sentences will be better accepted than one long one. Give the reader a break. Feed him/her the information in small bites with a period after each bite. You know of course the best way to eat an elephant -- one bite at a time.

Regarding adjectives and adverbs, use them to startle, surprise, please, and wake up your reader when he/she least expects it. Use adjectives they would normally not expect to see in front of a word or phrase. Use adverbs only to carry the story forward, never as a clever way to extend your sentence. Think of them as seasoning in cooking. Too much spoils the dish.

By all means, in general, do not repeat the same nouns in the same paragraph. It is wise also to avoid using the same verb repeatedly in a paragraph. The mark of a good writer is the ability to intersperse various words that tell the story, instead of repeating the same descriptive nouns or verbs over and over again. Use synonyms generously.

Mix up longer sentences and shorter sentences. Particularly, following a necessary long sentence, punch your reader with a jab in the following sentence. Make it short.

Don't weave together a series of only short sentences though -- your book is not a Western Union telegram. Don't tire your reader either, with nothing but long, involved sentences. Remember you have permission to use as many sentences as need-be to make your point.

It is helpful, almost mandatory, to write as though you are talking to, or penning a letter to, a friend. Use the language you feel comfortable with. (Yes, that's a sentence that ends with a preposition. That's the way you would say it in conversation. It's okay to break some of the Victorian rules once in a while.)

Read out loud what you have written, and have someone else read it to you. If you find any awkward phrases, fix them so that the copy flows easily. You might want to record the manuscript yourself, in your own voice, and then listen to the playback. The whole idea is to make the book easy and comfortable to read.

Being creative means doing it your way. Being professional means following some fundamental rules that make it easy on your reader to absorb what you write. You need to be both --

creative, yet professional -- to give birth to a successful book.

You probably wrote your book with a feeling of free and easy mind-wandering. Now it's time though, to focus, and clean up the little details that make or break a good book.

Beginning and Ending

One of the important little details in writing is chapter endings. Each of your chapters must end with a sentence that motivates the reader to continue into the next chapter. Don't let him/her feel that the book ends here. The ending sentence does not need to pertain to the next chapter, but it can pertain to something to come later in the book. Tease them. Ask a question, generate a *yes-but*; let them know there are surprises to come later in the book. Use the chapter endings as bridges to make the book flow.

Even though you think the book is finished, you can go back and plug in these chapter endings, It will most likely be worth the effort.

The first chapter of a book is a gateway that must beckon the reader to proceed and read the rest of the book. Some authors put off writing the first chapter until the rest of the book is finished. One very successful best-selling author in the 1950's wrote a book that was absolutely bad -- no one could possibly enjoy reading it. However, he sat down and wrote, or maybe hired someone else to write, a steamy, explicitly sexy first page and first chapter that had absolutely nothing to do with the rest of the story. His book was published and became a best seller of the time. Who is to know how many people bought it because they quickly browsed the introduction, only to discover later they had purchased a lemon instead of a plum, or if they fell prey to misleading publicity about the book, or if they bought it solely because he was a well-known author.

That is not a recommendation for you to follow. It is only stated to emphasize the point that the first chapter is important.

The last chapter is the archway through which your reader exits your book. Make it attractive. Make him/her feel glad they read the book all the way through. It is the place to sum up, answer all the unanswered questions in the reader's mind, and make him/her feel it is okay to stop reading, realizing that this story has ended. It should also leave a satisfied, pleasant frame of mind in which to think back and remember what the book said. It is the place for closure.

If you end your novel's story but leave the reader wondering what happened to the characters he/she has become comfortable with envisioning, you may want to create an epilog.

Without an epilog, you can of course leave the reader breathless to read the next book in the series. A series, by its very nature, is a string of independent episodes involving the same main characters. Each individual episode must have an ending leaving the reader anxious to read the next installment.

Some authors find it difficult to write the last chapter in a book of fiction. They have many thoughts in mind about what might happen next to the book's characters. You don't usually kill off all your characters in the book. They will live on after you say THE END. Knowing this introduces doubt in your mind regarding how to walk away and leave them behind. You struggle and yearn to add just a little bit more to the story.

The way to overcome this doubt and hesitation is to think about the ending of this book as the closing of the door after you have visited someone in their home. You can always come back to see them again. You can write another novel framed to take place after the end of this book.

For non-fiction writers, the last chapter is not nearly so difficult. When you have finished saying what you want to say, you simply end the book. It did what you wanted it to do. It informed the reader. There is no concern about fictitious characters -- there aren't any.

The last chapter of the non-fiction book must nevertheless leave the reader with a satisfied feeling. Sometimes it makes sense to summarize what you have presented in the book in the form of a bulleted list.

Creative?

At this point you are logically asking *"What is the difference between creative writing and non-creative writing?"* One good way to think of the answer to this question is to define most non-fiction writing as simply putting a bunch of facts into written form. Skillful writing is necessary, but there is no imagination. No need to develop characters. No need for emotional involvement. No need for a story as such.

Creative fiction writing is just the opposite. Creative writing banks on calling up the reader's emotions. Some authors express it this way: Show -- Don't Tell (let the reader fill in a lot of details in his/her own mind -- assume they are going to create their own mental images).

On the other hand, a non-fiction book can be creatively written. In other words, you can write a book in a fashion that no one else has used. You can make the book a creative effort. You can use words in a creative fashion that will hold the reader's interest. Some authors use the technique of inventing two or more characters and have them tell the story through dialog.

Now, what about poetry? Here all the rules fly out the window. Your poetry is a combination of thoughts presented in an attractive format. You control when the reader goes to the next line. You present a chain of thoughts that will make the reader think. You presume he/she may go back several times and read your lines again. The grammatical rules of poetry do not exist. It's your show. Creative writing? You bet.

As well as non-fiction and fiction, poetry should be published for readers to enjoy it. Poetry readings are fine, but they reach a limited number of listeners. This book is about publishing, and poetry books are just as important to consider as fiction and non-fiction.

When you publish, you want the maximum number of people to read your work.

So, now that we have discussed a few of the subtleties and nuances that can improve your book and help you polish it to a shine of professionalism, let's delve into exactly how to publish your book.

Chapter 4

Publishing A Printed Book

There are two ways to publish your book as a printed book. One way is to seduce the good graces of a big publisher, recognizing the conditions and consequences mentioned in Chapter 1. The other way is to publish your book independently.

The first step in getting a big publisher to publish your book is to find an agent. Most of the big publishers will refuse to read or evaluate your manuscript without the participation of a recognized literary agent. Over the years, the literary agents across the United States have developed relationships with the big publishers and they have a good feeling for which publisher might be interested in your particular book. If the agent likes your book, he/she will submit it to one or more big publishers.

Finding an agent for yourself today involves first sending him/her a query via email. Lists of agents with their email address abound on the Internet, but most of the lists in printed books are obsolete and do not show an email address. A quick way to find such lists on the Internet is to type the words *literary agents* into Google. Often the list will show which genres and types of books each particular agent is interested in considering.

Gone are the days when you bundled up your typewritten manuscript and mailed it to first one agent, then another, and another, hoping they would read it and express an interest. There are only a scattered few agents who still work this way -- insisting on receiving a typewritten manuscript accompanied by the famous SASE -- a self-addressed stamped envelope.

Most of those old-style submissions resulted in a diplomatically worded rejection slip enclosed with your manuscript when they returned it to you after a few months, and most of the agents frowned upon simultaneous submissions to multiple agents, so the hunting process took many months, sometimes years. The process of finding an agent was slow and painful.

Ironically a few of the old-line, well respected agents who still work this way are successful in getting you a publishing contract with a Big Publisher.

Your Query

Agents are busy people. Time is their most valuable asset and the easier you make it for them to evaluate your book, the better for you. If they are turned off by your query style, they won't even spend the time to look further. It is a waste of time to create a fancy flowery description of your book. They've seen 'em all. They want to know what's in your book -- not what you think of it.

Nowadays most agents prefer that you send them an email query to start the ball rolling. When you send a query, you switch hats from creative author to sales person.

Included in the query email should be a very brief description of your book. The description blurb should be short, and part of the body of the actual email -- they may not take the time to open an attachment. It should state the genre of your book and present a quick take on exactly what the book is all about. The subject of the email should be "Query" so they will know what to expect.

The typical agent has a heavy backlog of queries to process every day. Thousands of authors are seeking agents. Your query email can make you or break you.

If you send a message that attracts their interest, they might respond with a request that you send them an excerpt from your book. This time an attached document is okay. Keep it short. Make it just long enough to capture their attention. If they feel your book is in their bailiwick of interest, quite often they will quickly request a specified number of pages, starting with Chapter One, to see if you write well enough to qualify as a serious candidate for publication.

Your job is to present the essence of the book -- the genre and to whom it is aimed -- its niche -- along with a brief set of words that tell what the book is about.

Most agents specialize in certain genres and in specific market segments. They keep in close touch with publishers who love to publish books about a particular subject matter or a certain type of reader, such as romance novels, how-to books, historical books, mystery, science fiction, children's books, etc. Just like the medical profession where most doctors are specialists and general practitioners are fewer, rare is the agent who could be classified as a general agent interested in everything.

Platform

Another thing both agents and publishers are very much interested in today is your "platform." By that they mean is have you already established a crowd of readers who love your books and tell their friends. They want to know how many books you have sold so far. Is this another book following your previous books. They are interested in the marketing of the book, and particularly what you have done about marketing your previous efforts before contacting them.

For the most part, if you don't have a platform, your chances of catching their attention is diminished severely. Thus, if you are a first time author, the field of agents who will give you the time of day narrows sharply.

Nevertheless, there are hundreds of honest, professional agents who are looking for fresh material to present to publishers. If you want a big publisher deal, by all means query a number of agents. You can query a lot of them at the same time, realizing that most of them will not be interested in your book.

If the agent likes what he/she sees in your brief blurb and requests a bigger sample of your book, you are on the first step of procuring an agent. When he/she asks for a substantial part of the book, reads it and then requests the entire book, you are well on your way to becoming a client of that agent. Then, if he/she likes the whole book, you will get a phone call or an email offering you the opportunity to sign up with them as a link to actually finding a publisher.

By the way, if an agent asks for money from you up front, run the other way. There are charlatans advertising heavily on the Internet who charge you for taking a look. They pump you up with praise about your book and promise to submit it to multiple publishers. When you send them money, that's about the end of it. Many of them do nothing to expose your book to any publisher.

In today's digital world very few publishers ask the agent for a heavy, typed manuscript to be submitted, so there are no longer printing and mailing costs. All legitimate ethical agents evaluate your work and go to work for you at no charge. They make their money through commissions on each sale, in the same manner you make money from royalties. They want your book to be a success so they will make more money.

Sounds a bit exhausting so far, doesn't it. Well, you have only cracked the surface at this point.

Most agents will contact their insider friends at one or two publishing houses in New York and suggest they take a look. If there is no interest, they might turn to their second tier of publishers -- those who might want your genre or special interest, but who are not constant companions with this particular agent.

If too many publishers turn them down, they then turn you down.

What you want is a diligent agent who likes your book and really wants to sell it to a publisher. The story about J. K. Rowling, perhaps the most successful author in the world, being turned down by scores of agents and publishers is true. Without diligence, she never would have made the fortune she has accumulated writing about Harry Potter. She finally found an agent who felt her books would sell, and he convinced a publisher. The rest is history.

In extraordinary circumstances the team of agent and publisher representative might move forward right away to talk about a contract if the publisher also likes your book. This happens when a celebrity decides to publish a book. Publishers compete to sign the celebrity. The celebrity's book goes to the head of the line, even ahead of the best-selling authors. Your book trails behind these two priority groups.

More likely, if the agent loves your book, he/she will hold on to it until the once-a-year big meeting they have in New York each summer, where lots of agents formally pitch their books to a room full of publishers. You will not be invited. At this gathering, the publishers choose, from the many books presented to them, the ones they will seriously consider. After reviewing all those first round choices, they then decide which ones to publish next year. Afterwards they tell the agent nay or okay. Then the agent and the publisher negotiate a contract for you, and the agent presents it to you. It's a cherished procedure that has been in place for many years, and it is unlikely to be abandoned anytime soon.

During the time between when an agent agrees to become your agent and he/she actually negotiates a contract with the publisher, your agent may go to work making a detail evaluation of your book. He/she may put a professional editor to work going over your work with a fine tooth comb. The agent and the editor will make suggestions about changing the book if they feel the changes will create a better likelihood of a publisher saying yes. It is in your best interests to seriously consider the changes they might recommend, even though your author's pride might tempt you to take offense that they want to tinker with your masterpiece.

After a publisher issues a contract, one or more editors will enter the scene and work closely with you to "improve" the book. You may or may not agree with their suggested changes, but remember, after you get a signed contract with a conventional publisher, the publisher rules. You no longer own the book.

After you sign a contract with the big publisher, they will send you a cash advance. The amount of the advance varies at their pleasure. A few thousand dollars is the rule of thumb. They are in the gambling game, so they decide how much to ante up depending upon their idea of how well your book might sell.

The publisher then puts a staff of people to work. They design a cover. They design the inside layout, choose the type fonts, and change the content of the book at their will. They set in motion a professional advertising and promotional program, often months in advance of the actual publication date (in order to build up anticipation and enthusiasm prior to actual publication). They try to get publicity exposure for you the author.

After they gather feedback about what the market might be, they decide how many books to print on the first run.

Then the fun begins. Before publication date the publisher -- via your agent -- may ask you to go around the nation appearing on radio or TV shows, speaking to groups of readers. This continues after publication. They schedule book signings for you. They put a professional effort into trying to get a lot of people to buy your book. They apply pressure on book stores to order your book according to the publisher's terms.

They want your book to be a success.

They carefully monitor sales and acceptance for two or three months after the book's release. If sales soar, they print more books and may continue promotional efforts. If, on the other hand, the book does not sell well enough -- based on their accounting department's projections and formula -- they will decide within about three or four months to yank the book from circulation. They retrieve all unsold copies of the book and recycle the paper. They don't want copies of your discontinued book taking up valuable space in their warehouse. Your book is a corpse and there is absolutely nothing you can do about it.

Many authors have learned all this the hard way.

If your book does sell well and your royalties roll in, congratulations. If not, you have just completed another course in the College of Hard Knocks.

Should you ply the path of agent/big publisher? It's entirely up to you. It's a gamble. If you feel confident that your book will be a big seller right away, and if you are willing to live with the results, good or bad, by all means go ahead. If a big publisher does accept your book, they will spend a lot of time and money to promote it. If you publish it independently, you will have to spend time and money yourself to promote your book and/or hire a professional to do the work, but you will still own the copyright if and when it doesn't set the world on fire immediately upon publication.

Chapter 5

Independent Publishing

As an alternative to seducing a big publisher, you may choose to go the route of independent publishing. The recommended way to publish your book as a conventional printed book these days -- hardbound and/or paperback -- is to engage the services and facilities of an independent publishing company. (The term indie is often used to describe such a publishing company or even more frequently to describe an author who chooses to publish independently.)

If you decide to publish independently you don't need an agent. You deal directly with the publisher. The independent publishers are quite willing to deal with you directly, over the Internet. As time goes by, a new breed of agents will very likely find a way to get involved, between you and the publishers.

The old line publishers own your book. The indies do not; you own it.

The indie publishers do not review your book and make suggestions about how to change it (unless, of course, you pay them extra to do so). They simply print what you send them. That is one of the key differences between old line big publishers and independent publishing.

At present the independent publishers don't do any promotion unless your book sales soar as a result of your own promotion.

Promotional agencies exist, to help you market your published book.

There are three types of companies in business to help you publish your book independently. All of the substantial ones advertise on the Internet, and they have websites explaining exactly what they do.

One group of companies, offers a complete range of services.

Another group will print your books on demand in any quantity whenever you want some.

The third group prints books in the old fashion manner, meaning they only print a lot of books at a time and send them to you.

Some companies advertise themselves under the heading "self-publishing" if you search the web. However, they only offer the service of printing your book. They are not really publishers. They are essentially only printers. They print books and ship them to you. They do nothing to set up distribution for you. It is your responsibility to sell the books and deliver them to customers.

The more books you buy at a time, the lower the cost per book. Some authors choose this route, order hundreds of books, store them, and wait for the sales to come in. This is not a good business model for most authors. The only situation that favors such low cost volume printing is when you plan to sell your non-fiction books at seminars *etc*. The cost per book to you may be less with the companies that print large quantities at a time, but overall the disadvantages of using this system of marketing your book usually outweigh the cost per book advantages.

Each of the genuine independent publishing companies offers a cafeteria menu of services. In their Premium Packages they will take your raw document file, which you send them via email, and perform the entire publication process to completion. They will design a custom book cover, or you can choose one of their standard templates at little or no cost. They will design the book's interior and print a proof copy for you to review. No longer galley proofs. You see the finished product for your proof reading.

After your approval they are ready right away to print and ship any number of books -- from one to many. They arrange to perform the complete fulfillment function -- meaning they will take orders and ship books to anyone, including yourself, only after they receive an order.

They also offer you optional editing services and optional marketing and promotion packages, but they don't promote much. They just provide the tools for use in marketing your book, such as posters, post cards, bookmarks, business cards, *etc.* They may send out a press release for you, but for the most part they are not marketing professionals.

Importantly, the independent publishing company will provide an ISBN number and barcode logo, and list your book with all the major distributors of books. Retail sellers and libraries buy from the distributors, from wholesalers, or directly from the publisher. Most of them insist on the ISBN number to order and keep track of books.

The indie publisher will print and ship books directly to the distributors and resellers, collect the money from the purchasers and send you royalties. Most of them will also honor and process direct orders for one or more books from retail customers, and ship them promptly, often overnight. The Print On Demand system made possible by today's

49

computers eliminates the need for warehousing thousands of printed books. When someone (including you) orders one or more books they print the books, and then ship them.

Using digital computer systems, they store only the original digital computer file of your book and then print any number of copies when a sale is made. This is a tremendous advantage to you because it lowers their expenses and they can pass the savings on to you.

Another minor advantage is that you can make changes to your book at any time after initial publication for a very modest cost, and provide an updated edition almost immediately.

If you choose, the publishers will provide only some of these services and you take care of the rest. This way, you can control the costs of publishing and promoting.

If you want to be just an author, and not a production coordinator and marketing person, you will want to buy their full package of services, and also hire yourself a good promotion agency. You should consider engaging the services of a book marketing professional to actually promote your book -- someone with a good track record.

Each publisher has its unique requirements for the computer file you send them. If you are comfortable with your computer and the esoteric features of Microsoft Word, and making PDF and HTML files, you yourself can do a big portion of what they offer to do for you.

Most independent publishers prefer to receive your finished manuscript document via transmission over email. Most of them accept files created by Microsoft Word. A few will accept other file formats including PDF and HTML.

If you don't use Microsoft Word, you may have to convert your file into Word format in order to optimize their system of publishing.

If you don't know how to convert a manuscript file produced by a word processing program other than Word, some publishers and other independent professionals will do the conversion for you, at a price.

The question arises, how should you set up your word processor to format your manuscript to send to the publisher. Single or double space, margins, type font, indentation, page numbering or not, headers and footers -- all the formatting you used to create your work. The requirements are specified by the publisher. Each publisher has its own requirements.

All in all, it's a straightforward process getting your printed book independently published.

Chapter 6

Publishing An E-book

You really should publish your book as an E-book, whether you publish it as a printed book or not. The optimum is to publish both. Some people prefer to read printed books, some like E-books.

Some authors choose to publish an E-book to start with and see what happens. If the book sells well, they then publish a printed version of the book. There are three reasons for doing this.

First, the cost of publishing an E-book is tremendously less than publishing a printed book.

Second, if some typos or other errors show up, or you discover that a few modifications in your E-book will improve its marketability, it is painless to make the changes in the E-book. Changing a printed book is much more complicated and expensive.

Third, if your E-book sells well, you have a platform to present to a big publisher agent.

First of all, regarding costs -- publishing an E-book after you have produced a proper digital manuscript can be modest, or even zero. That's a powerful statement, but it is true. Yes, that's right, zero. The leading E-book publisher Smashwords will indeed publish your book at no cost. Their service consists of converting your file into multiple different formats that can be read by all the leading E-book readers. This includes versions that anyone can read on any desktop or laptop.

Smashwords is a new type of company that has grown at a fantastic rate during the last few years. It acts as both a publisher and a basic distributor for your E-book. They do not publish printed books, (although they have a sister company that does). They place your book with all the major E-book sellers except Amazon at the time of this writing.

There is a possibility that even the almighty Amazon will eventually come around and agree to a contract to accept books from Smashwords. Amazon holds out for special terms and conditions, based on the fact that at this time it is the world's largest book seller. Meantime, Barnes & Noble, Apple, Sony, Kobo, Diesel and other E-book sellers have agreed to sell books produced by Smashwords.

Not to worry, Amazon will also accept your book as a computer file directly from you, and convert it into the format that can be read on their Kindle E-readers. They will then stock your book and sell it, remitting royalties directly to you. There is a minimal charge for publishing your E-book at this time. They do not care if you also publish it with someone else. Amazon also publishes printed books as well as E-books. They act as an independent publisher for both.

This book was published as an E-book by Smashwords, and also separately by Amazon for the Kindle.

Other small and independent book publishers, who have been publishing printed books for a long time, are now offering to convert your printed book into an E-book for a few hundred dollars if they publish your printed book. Various publishers offer various ways to get your E-books into the hands of distributors.

Some of the pioneer independent publishers, who depend upon older, conventional printing methods, have been swiftly left behind in both printed and E-books. The technology of today allows newcomers to get into business fast, and offer more features and/or better costs than the publishing companies that have been around a long time and have heavy investment in conventional printing and binding equipment. An E-book publisher needs only a small office and an excellent computer system.

The jury is not in regarding what the Big Publishers will do regarding E-books. They have been fighting the whole idea of E-books so far, at the time this book is written. They have many millions invested in equipment, warehouse space, and expensive office space in New York.

It is inevitable that they will come up with a solution to their dilemma. The dilemma is that E-books now outsell printed books on Amazon, and the separation is growing rapidly. They cannot afford to ignore E-books.

E-book publishers can sell E-books at very low prices compared to printed books. This is because an E-book publisher does not need an expensive office in Manhattan, a large warehouse for storing books, and agents who take a percentage of sales income. As a result, E-book publishers offer royalties remarkably higher than traditional conventional printed book royalties. The typical E-book royalty is seventy or eighty percent of the cover price. This is a god-send for authors.

When you publish your E-book independently, you set the book price. If you crunch the numbers it becomes apparent that if you offer an E-book for a low price (say less than five dollars) the royalty income you receive exceeds the royalties for printed books, by a wide margin. It costs the publishers a lot of money to manufacture and ship a printed book, whether it be hard cover or soft cover. It costs the E-book publisher nothing to deliver a book except a few seconds of computer downloading time, which is done automatically.

If you have your book published as a printed book, the question arises should you have the price of your book printed on the cover. It's up to you. Remember prices in general in today's economy change. In the case of E-books you can change the price whenever you like, as often as you like. Printed books with the price shown on the cover cannot be changed easily.

Low-priced E-books by new authors in general outsell books priced above five dollars. Some established best selling authors' E-books are priced higher, and they still get the high percentage royalties. Many best selling authors have discovered this and are now publishing both printed books and E-books.

There is one disadvantage in letting the publisher produce both a printed book and an E-book. Most of them that offer the combination service will not place the E-book with all the sources to resell your book in the proper format for certain specific E-readers. This includes Amazon, which offers the service. Amazon publishes only in the format for the Kindle reader.

It is vital that you compare the exact services provided by the various E-book publishers in order to assure the widest possible circulation of your book.

Formatting Your E-book

When you write a book and produce a computer file, you would normally think to format the book with printed pages in mind. Page numbers, margins, typeface, and overall appearance are taken into account.

Beware. An E-book is not a printed book. The correct format for a file that will be turned into an E-book must literally ignore some of the rules of the road for printed books. An E-book will be read on various types of electronic reading devices, each one a little different from the others. You must omit page numbers. You dare not use a fancy type face. You don't control the type size displayed -- the person using the E-reader sets his/her own preference of type size.

Technical requirements for an E-book file are strict. A computer will be reading your file, not a human being, and computers are ruthless in following certain procedures such as page formatting.

Even for a printed book, the format of the computer file you send to the Print on Demand publisher must follow certain rules, but for an E-book, the rules are much stricter. An E-book is a different animal from a printed book. For a printed book, your computer file will be converted by the publisher into a format to operate their own printing equipment. In many cases, the E-book publisher must convert to multiple formats.

The finished files which the publisher produces must conform to the technical requirements of each of the E-book formats in use.

The formats at this time include Epub, RTF, LRF, PDP, HTML, Rich Text, MOBI, PDF, Kindle, and plain text. As time goes by, no doubt even more technical formats will evolve in new products. You want your book to show up well in all these formats. It is the job of the publisher to assure that.

Fonts & Image Sizes Important

One of the things to keep in mind about E-books is that people will read them on all sizes of E-reader screens. The images will show up quite small on tiny E-readers. On a desktop or laptop, the images will be even larger than an ordinary printed book. The words and pictures must carry themselves in all the different sizes of readers.

So what should you as the author do to make it possible or easy for the publisher to perform accurate conversions for the many E-readers? The best overall answer to this question is KISS. The famous slogan Keep It Simple Stupid applies here. The simpler your book format is, the better. You can make it possible and even easy by conforming to a few simple rules.

Rule Number One demands that you quit thinking of a fancy layout for the pages of your book. Fancy layouts help in printed books. They make a book look distinctive. For E-books however, a consistent standard type face throughout the book is a must. No elaborate dropped capitals, boxes around chapter titles, or script faces. Sans serif type or one of the established faces like New Times Roman perform the best.

Rule Number Two is to think of the finished E-book as looking more like the old galley proofs than a printed book. The E-book reader scrolls down through your written masterpiece as though it was one long statement. You can break it into chapters of course, with chapter numbers displayed in a larger type size if desired, but the E-reader device decides how much to put on each page and what the margins are. The E-reader does not want you to insert page breaks, or many carriage return spaces, or blank pages before jumping into the next chapter, as a printed book normally does.

In some respects, it is easier on the author to write for an E-book instead of a printed book. There is little you can do to influence how the book is presented to the reader -- the computer decides. As a result, you can just sit down and write a long treatise without even thinking about how it will look when displayed.

Microsoft Word is the preferred word processing program to use when submitting a book file to most E-book publishers unless they tell you otherwise. Their computer systems are optimized to read files produced by that program, which happens to be the most popular program in use.

The Microsoft Word program, though, has some quirks that can trip you up. It often inserts hidden commands regarding the format of your book. To properly format a file for conversion to an E-book, it is usually necessary to "clean up the file" before sending it off to the publisher. If the file does not perform satisfactorily, the publisher will bounce it back to you for modification. This frustrates many authors who pay no attention to the special formatting requirements. The solution is, if you are not completely comfortable cleaning up the Word file to the publishers' satisfaction, there are professionals who will perform the task at very reasonable rates.

What about pictures, drawings, graphs, and tables? Yes, you can include graphic images in an E-book, but the task becomes extremely tedious and difficult it you try to create tables and position them beside graphic images. Again, each publisher has different requirements for converting your manuscript into E-books. It is wise to investigate the requirements and probabilities for successful conversion. A text-only novel is the easiest form to convert.

Time To Take Action

You have put a lot of time into producing your manuscript so far. After reading this book, and hopefully following the suggestions for polishing, it is time to act -- go ahead and publish it! The world awaits your words.

######

About the Author:

Henry Jordan (aka Hank Jordan) lives in Southern California with his wife Eleanor. He started serious writing as editor of his third grade and high school newspapers. Active in editing and publishing for many years, he has published several magazines, weekly newspapers, and books -- both fiction and non-fiction. He also founded and managed four different businesses during his adult life – an advertising agency, an aircraft dealership, a computer systems company, and a business consultancy. These days he writes some free lance material and he is well into his next novel. He operates Hank10 Publishing Co., which publishes books (including this one) and offers editing, publishing and creative writing consulting. You can find out more about the author at http://www.hankjordan.com.

Dear Reader:

If you enjoyed this book, and/or found it useful, please tell your friends, and then go to the site where you purchased it and post a review.

#